Recovery

A Coaching Workbook

Cortney Lovell

Our Wellness Collective Printing

The Valatie Professional Building
1052 Kinderhook Street
Valatie, NY 12184

www.OurWellnessCollective.com

Copyright © 2018 Cortney Lovell

All rights reserved. No part of this work may be reproduced or used in any form by any means, graphic, electronic or mechanical, including but not limited to photocopying, recording or taping or any other means of information storage and retrieval system, without the prior expressed written permission of the author.

Printed in the United States of America.

Contents

Nah, not me..before you began

Well, maybe..when you got this book

Yeah, so what now?..the beginning of this book

Let's do it!...all of this book

It really is possible...every day ahead

To those who are suffering.

To those who are no longer here to walk this journey.

To all of the versions of ourselves we are leaving behind.

To the person we are in this moment, brave enough to become someone new.

If you're holding this book then chances are you have made a decision to explore recovery and dive into the diverse waters of wellness, or the universe is offering you a very big nudge. By whatever means you have come to be reading these words, welcome.

The process of recovering from anything can be daunting. The tasks of unlearning deeply embedded behaviors, unraveling engrained habits, and re-wiring automatic reactions to stimuli could seem like an impossible feat. As overwhelming as these changes might seem, they are possible.

recovery is possible

we are all recovering from something

from something

OR MANY THINGS

You are one rain drop in the same river we are all flowing through. The only difference is, the scenery along your current shoreline might be a bit different from the next. Our perspectives might vary, but we are all on the same journey of life.

Recognizing change needs to be made in your life is an important part of the recovery process. It is healthy to step back, assess what is and is not working, and start fresh.

In the space below, write out your ideas of a fresh start. What are the things that need to be trimmed and what needs to be watered?

Compassion

How does compassion help others to heal?
_____
_____
_____
_____
_____
_____
_____
_____

How does love help us to heal?
_____
_____
_____
_____
_____
_____
_____
_____

Love

breathe deeply

try this

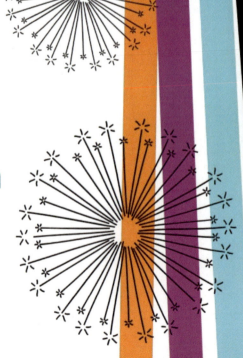

diaphragmatic breathing exercise

rest one hand over your chest and the other over your belly button

take a deep breath in

breathe in until the hand over your belly raises slightly, followed by the hand over your chest

repeat 10x

"Where does the breeze end and the breath begin?"

Leonard Perlmutter (Ram Lev)

WHO ARE YOU?

Underneath all of the titles, the things, the attributes, who are you? If you were to remove all of the attachments we hold onto and often use to define us, who is left? Use the two spaces below to contemplate you.

What are those attachments you cling to? What are the titles or qualities you define yourself by? (Parent, student, teacher, lawyer, ambitious, kind, hard worker, etc.)

Who are you when you detach from all of these things?

WHERE WILL YOUR *journey* TAKE YOU?

Where is it that you want to end up? When will you know you've reached your recovery wellness goals?

If you look through a window into yourself, what will you see?

JoHari's Window is a method developed by two American psychologists, Joseph Luft and Harry Ingham. The exercise was created for individuals to visualize and understand themselves, as well as their relationships with others. This tool will help you to inventory your personal characteristics from both inside and outside perspectives.

Open Window

This first window pane contains information, or descriptions, known to both yourself and others.

Blind Window

This window pane holds the things known to others, but not yet to yourself. This ranges from small matters outside your self-awareness, to deep issues that are observable to others, but you remain blind to.

Hidden Window

This window pane is known to you, but not to others. It contains secrets intentionally hidden, and private information you have not yet shared.

Unknown Window

The final window pane contains information about yourself that neither you nor others are aware of yet.

Try this

In the space provided in the window panes on the next page, fill in five things about yourself that are in your Open window, and five things about yourself that are in your Hidden window.

Suggestion

As you work through your Recovery Wellness Coaching Plan, add things to your Blind Window and your Unknown window as you become aware of them. Can you find five things to fit into each window pane on your journey?

HOW DO WE CONNECT WITH OURSELVES AND OTHERS?

ALWAYS REMAIN CURIOUS

OPEN-ENDED QUESTIONS INVITE AN INDIVIDUAL TO TELL THEIR OWN STORY

if we ask good questions and remain genuinely curious of the answers, we are creating space for others to hold power

QUESTIONS TO CONSIDER

1) HOW HAS THAT WORKED OUT FOR YOU?

2) WHAT HAS WORKED IN THE PAST?

3) WHAT COULD I DO TO SUPPORT YOU?

4) WHAT DO YOU THINK THE NEXT STEP IS?

5) WHAT ARE YOUR THOUGHTS?

6) WHAT IS DIFFERENT THIS TIME?

7) WOULD YOU TELL ME MORE ABOUT THAT?

8) WHAT DOES THAT MEAN TO YOU?

9) HOW DO YOU SEE YOURSELF ACCOMPLISHING THIS?

10) HOW DO YOU DEFINE YOUR RECOVERY?

Would you share about your personal definition of **recovery**? Where did it come from?

DISCOVER WHAT FILLS THE PAGES OF YOUR STORY

Welcome to the next chapter in your story. What will you write?

If you look back over the course of our life you can usually divide your life up into different stages or chapters. Think back over your life and try to identify how many major chapters you have already cycled through. _____

AND YOU WILL BE WHO YOU INTEND TO BE

what are you grateful for?

start out by writing ten things you are grateful for. as you work through your recovery wellness journey and identify other things to be grateful for, add them to this page. how long will it take you to fill the page?

IN ORDER TO FILL THE PAGES OF OUR NEW STORY, WE MUST TAKE THE TIME FOR DAILY

REFLECTIONS

TRY TO FILL A FULL PAGE A DAY FOR SEVEN DAYS TODAY IS PRACTICE. LET YOUR THOUGHTS FLOW.

DON'T THINK. JUST WRITE.

_____
_____
_____
_____
_____
_____
_____
_____
_____
_____
_____
_____
_____
_____

DON'T THINK. JUST WRITE.

DON'T THINK. JUST WRITE.

DON'T THINK. JUST WRITE.

DON'T THINK. JUST WRITE.

DON'T THINK. JUST WRITE.

DON'T THINK. JUST WRITE.

DON'T THINK. JUST WRITE.

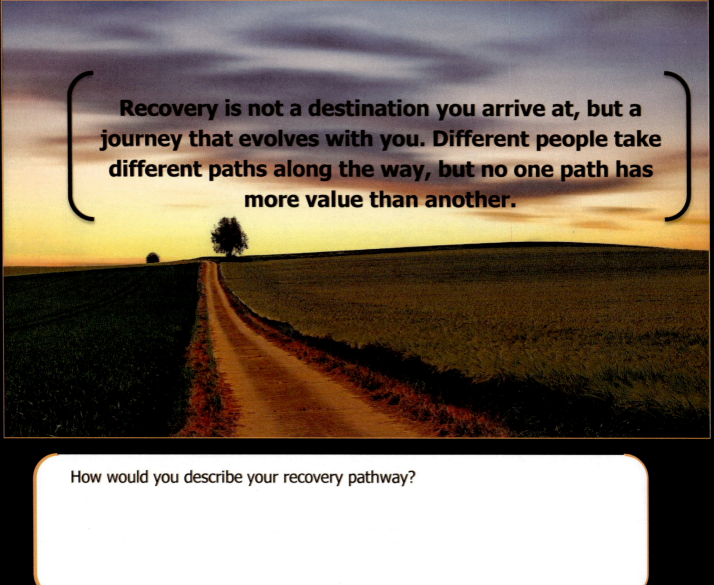

Recovery is not a destination you arrive at, but a journey that evolves with you. Different people take different paths along the way, but no one path has more value than another.

How would you describe your recovery pathway?

What are things you have tried already to support your recovery process?

What are things you haven't yet tried, but would like to?

Target your Wellness

The scene
When we are under pressure our vision can sometimes close so narrow we only see the worrisome thing directly in front of us. This type of tunnel vision can increase our stress levels and the likelihood of returning back to behaviors we are trying to change.

On our recovery journey it is helpful to expand our vision as broadly as we can to have a clearer perspective of the bigger picture. If our vision is focused on our *purpose,* we can use techniques to keep us grounded in the *present* moment and our *perspective* can become something we use to our advantage, no matter how stressful the journey becomes.

Target your Wellness

Try this
1) In the center most circle above, identify what *your purpose* on your recovery journey is. Not only the reason you want to change the behaviors and habit patterns, but what you feel called to do with the rest of your story beyond this chapter.
2) In the second circle, write in some techniques to help you ground yourself in *your present journey*.
    (I.E. deep breathing, meditation, yoga, writing, etc.)
3) In the outer most circle, describe your perspective of the healthiest version of yourself and your life in recovery.

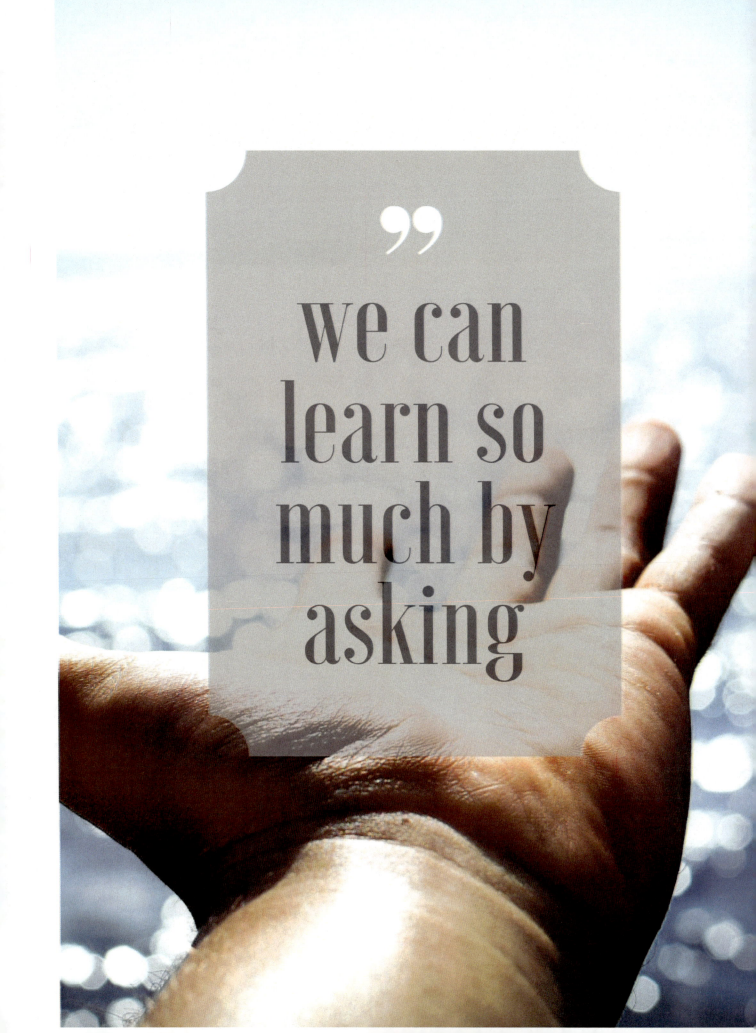

INDIVIDUALLY WE ACCOMPLISH GREAT THINGS

Who are five people you consider to be on your team?

1.

2.

3.

4.

5.

BUT TOGETHER, WE CAN ACCOMPLISH THE IMPOSSIBLE

find the resources in everyone

Everyone is their own best resource. Sometimes, we need someone to believe in our resources so we can begin to see the value ourselves.

Think of someone you know who appears to be living the kind of life you would like and describe five characteristics or qualities they possess that are resources for their success.

1.

2.

3.

4.

5.

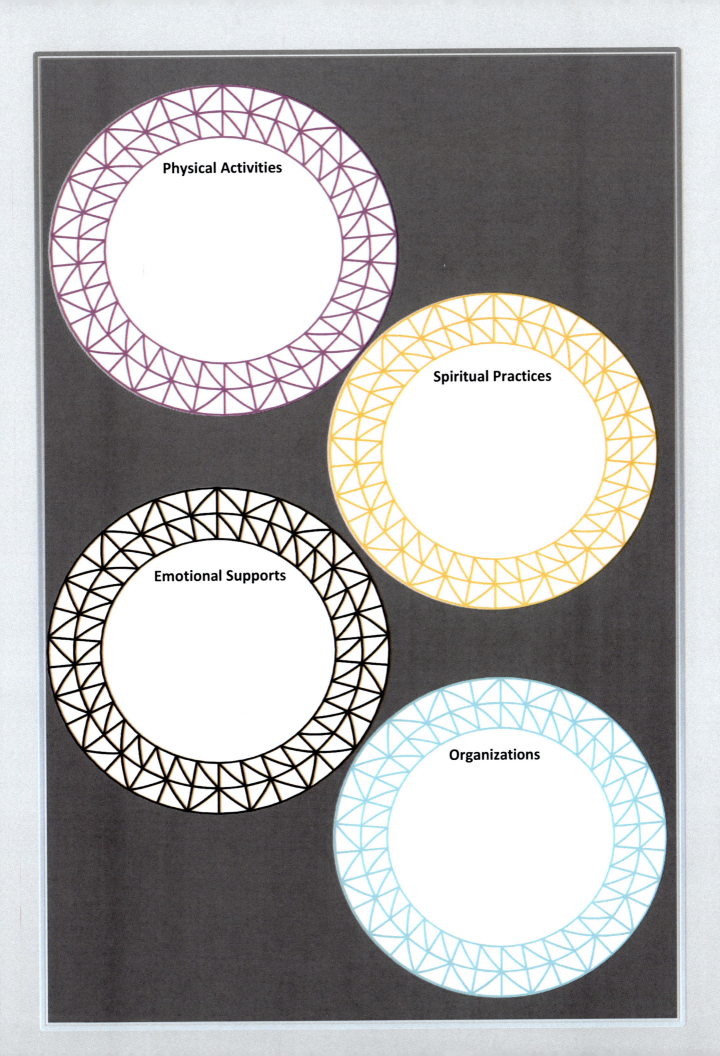

TO ME, FROM ME

TRY THIS

use only these two pages
pick an age younger than 13
write yourself a letter from the
perspective you have now
what would you tell yourself?

_____
_____
_____
_____
_____
_____
_____
_____
_____

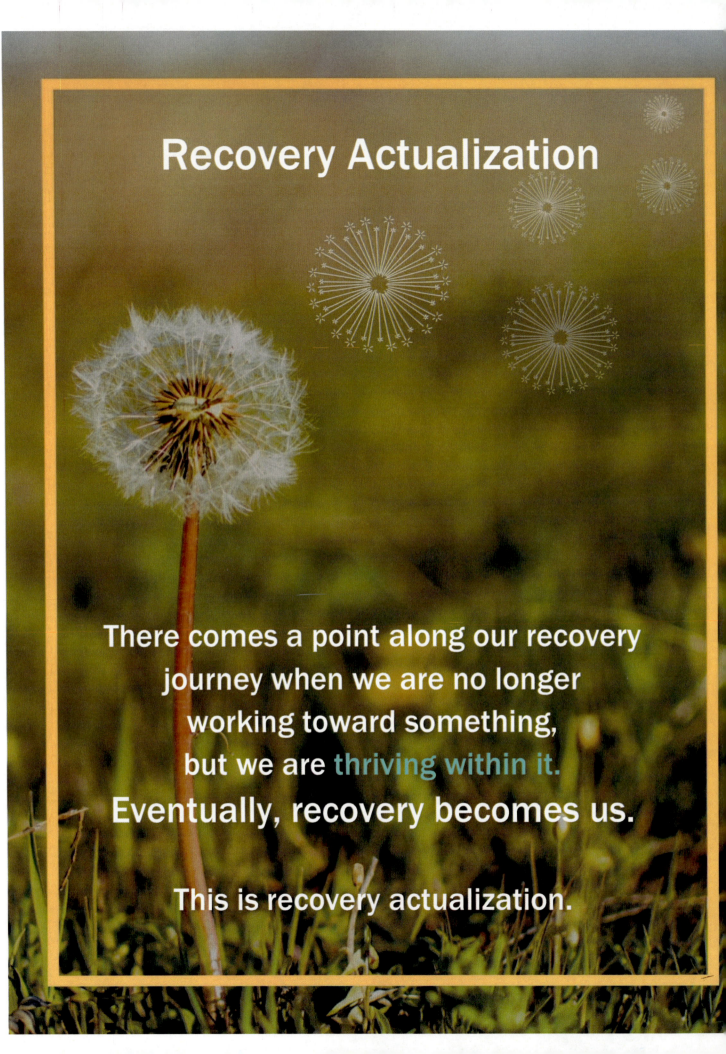

VISUALIZATION

try this

Find a safe, quite place to sit or lay down

Close your eyes and take 10 deep, diaphragmatic breaths

Allow an image of yourself to come to mind

Visualize yourself as the person you will be when you reach your recovery actualization stage

Who do you see?

Do you remember a difficult time when you felt truly supported by another person?

What was the scenario? Why was it a difficult time?

Who supported you?

Why did you feel supported? What did the individual do for you?

COMPASSION IN ACTION

Describe what it means to have someone truly walk with you on your recovery journey. How does it feel? What does it look like? Where do you go? Who walks with you?

_____
_____
_____
_____
_____
_____
_____
_____
_____

IS TO WALK WITH ANOTHER ON THEIR JOURNEY TO WELLNESS

Your Personal Recovery Wellness Coaching Plan

The Recovery Wellness Coaching Plan is a tool used for setting and achieving goals within different domains to sustain positive lifestyle changes.

- The plan is for you to use independently or in collaboration with a coach
- It is up to you to write and maintain this plan
- A Recovery Wellness Coaching Plan provides a framework for recovery coaching

Wellness Area	See suggested areas below		
Goal	What do I want to work on for my recovery wellness?		
Why this goal?	Why do I want to accomplish this?		
	What is important about this?		
	What about this will help my wellness?		
My Resources	Supportive people	Supportive places	Programs
	Strengths	Strengths	Strengths
My action steps	How do I get started?	Do I need to reach out for help?	Is there something I need?
	Should things be removed?	Do I need to do research?	What's next?
When will I reach my goal?	When do you want to accomplish this by?		

Each wellness area can be filled in as needed. If you have more goals in one area, you can use multiple boxes for the same wellness area with various goals. Or, you could use one page per wellness area.

Here are twelve suggestions of wellness areas to identify goals for:

Overall Recovery & Wellness	Spiritual / Purpose	Emotional	Community / Connectedness
Family / Relationship	Job / Career	Physical	Financial
Continuing Education	Living Environment	Recreational / Hobby	Other

RECOVERY WELLNESS COACHING PLAN

Wellness Area:

What is my goal?

Why is this my goal?

What are my action steps?

What are my resources?

When do I want to reach my goal by?

Other Thoughts:

Suggested Wellness Areas:

- Overall Recovery & Wellness
- Spiritual / Purpose
- Emotional
- Community / Connection
- Family / Relationship
- Job / Career
- Physical
- Financial
- Continuing Education
- Living Environment
- Recreational / Hobby
- Other

RECOVERY WELLNESS COACHING PLAN

Suggested Wellness Areas:

Overall Recovery & Wellness
Spiritual / Purpose
Emotional
Community / Connection
Family / Relationship
Job / Career
Physical
Financial
Continuing Education
Living Environment
Recreational / Hobby
Other

Wellness Area:

What is my goal?

Why is this my goal?

What are my action steps?

What are my resources?

When do I want to reach my goal by?

Other Thoughts:

RECOVERY WELLNESS COACHING PLAN

Wellness Area:

What is my goal?

Why is this my goal?

What are my action steps?

What are my resources?

When do I want to reach my goal by?

Other Thoughts:

Suggested Wellness Areas:

- Overall Recovery & Wellness
- Spiritual / Purpose
- Emotional
- Community / Connection
- Family / Relationship
- Job / Career
- Physical
- Financial
- Continuing Education
- Living Environment
- Recreational / Hobby
- Other

RECOVERY WELLNESS COACHING PLAN

Suggested Wellness Areas:

- Overall Recovery & Wellness
- Spiritual / Purpose
- Emotional
- Community / Connection
- Family / Relationship
- Job / Career
- Physical
- Financial
- Continuing Education
- Living Environment
- Recreational / Hobby
- Other

Wellness Area:

What is my goal?

Why is this my goal?

What are my action steps?

What are my resources?

When do I want to reach my goal by?

Other Thoughts:

RECOVERY WELLNESS COACHING PLAN

Wellness Area:

What is my goal?

Why is this my goal?

What are my action steps?

What are my resources?

When do I want to reach my goal by?

Other Thoughts:

Suggested Wellness Areas:

- Overall Recovery & Wellness
- Spiritual / Purpose
- Emotional
- Community / Connection
- Family / Relationship
- Job / Career
- Physical
- Financial
- Continuing Education
- Living Environment
- Recreational / Hobby
- Other

RECOVERY WELLNESS COACHING PLAN

Suggested Wellness Areas:

- Overall Recovery & Wellness
- Spiritual / Purpose
- Emotional
- Community / Connection
- Family / Relationship
- Job / Career
- Physical
- Financial
- Continuing Education
- Living Environment
- Recreational / Hobby
- Other

Wellness Area:

What is my goal?

Why is this my goal?

What are my action steps?

What are my resources?

When do I want to reach my goal by?

Other Thoughts:

RECOVERY WELLNESS COACHING PLAN

Wellness Area:

What is my goal?

Why is this my goal?

What are my action steps?

What are my resources?

When do I want to reach my goal by?

Other Thoughts:

Suggested Wellness Areas:

- Overall Recovery & Wellness
- Spiritual / Purpose
- Emotional
- Community / Connection
- Family / Relationship
- Job / Career
- Physical
- Financial
- Continuing Education
- Living Environment
- Recreational / Hobby
- Other

RECOVERY WELLNESS COACHING PLAN

Suggested Wellness Areas:

Overall Recovery & Wellness
Spiritual / Purpose
Emotional
Community / Connection
Family / Relationship
Job / Career
Physical
Financial
Continuing Education
Living Environment
Recreational / Hobby
Other

Wellness Area:

What is my goal?

Why is this my goal?

What are my action steps?

What are my resources?

When do I want to reach my goal by?

Other Thoughts:

RECOVERY WELLNESS COACHING PLAN

Wellness Area:

What is my goal?

Why is this my goal?

What are my action steps?

What are my resources?

When do I want to reach my goal by?

Other Thoughts:

Suggested Wellness Areas:

- Overall Recovery & Wellness
- Spiritual / Purpose
- Emotional
- Community / Connection
- Family / Relationship
- Job / Career
- Physical
- Financial
- Continuing Education
- Living Environment
- Recreational / Hobby
- Other

RECOVERY WELLNESS COACHING PLAN

Suggested Wellness Areas:

- Overall Recovery & Wellness
- Spiritual / Purpose
- Emotional
- Community / Connection
- Family / Relationship
- Job / Career
- Physical
- Financial
- Continuing Education
- Living Environment
- Recreational / Hobby
- Other

Wellness Area:

What is my goal?

Why is this my goal?

What are my action steps?

What are my resources?

When do I want to reach my goal by?

Other Thoughts:

RECOVERY WELLNESS COACHING PLAN

Wellness Area:

What is my goal?

Why is this my goal?

What are my action steps?

What are my resources?

When do I want to reach my goal by?

Other Thoughts:

Suggested Wellness Areas:

- Overall Recovery & Wellness
- Spiritual / Purpose
- Emotional
- Community / Connection
- Family / Relationship
- Job / Career
- Physical
- Financial
- Continuing Education
- Living Environment
- Recreational / Hobby
- Other

RECOVERY WELLNESS COACHING PLAN

Suggested Wellness Areas:

- Overall Recovery & Wellness
- Spiritual / Purpose
- Emotional
- Community / Connection
- Family / Relationship
- Job / Career
- Physical
- Financial
- Continuing Education
- Living Environment
- Recreational / Hobby
- Other

Wellness Area:

What is my goal?

Why is this my goal?

What are my action steps?

What are my resources?

When do I want to reach my goal by?

Other Thoughts:

RECOVERY WELLNESS COACHING PLAN

Wellness Area:

What is my goal?

Why is this my goal?

What are my action steps?

What are my resources?

When do I want to reach my goal by?

Other Thoughts:

Suggested Wellness Areas:

- Overall Recovery & Wellness
- Spiritual / Purpose
- Emotional
- Community / Connection
- Family / Relationship
- Job / Career
- Physical
- Financial
- Continuing Education
- Living Environment
- Recreational / Hobby
- Other

RECOVERY WELLNESS COACHING PLAN

Suggested Wellness Areas:

- Overall Recovery & Wellness
- Spiritual / Purpose
- Emotional
- Community / Connection
- Family / Relationship
- Job / Career
- Physical
- Financial
- Continuing Education
- Living Environment
- Recreational / Hobby
- Other

What are my resources?

When do I want to reach my goal by?

Other Thoughts:

What are my action steps?

Wellness Area:

What is my goal?

Why is this my goal?

RECOVERY WELLNESS COACHING PLAN

Wellness Area:

What is my goal?

Why is this my goal?

What are my action steps?

What are my resources?

When do I want to reach my goal by?

Other Thoughts:

Suggested Wellness Areas:

- Overall Recovery & Wellness
- Spiritual / Purpose
- Emotional
- Community / Connection
- Family / Relationship
- Job / Career
- Physical
- Financial
- Continuing Education
- Living Environment
- Recreational / Hobby
- Other

RECOVERY WELLNESS COACHING PLAN

Suggested Wellness Areas:

Overall Recovery & Wellness
Spiritual / Purpose
Emotional
Community / Connection
Family / Relationship
Job / Career
Physical
Financial
Continuing Education
Living Environment
Recreational / Hobby
Other

Wellness Area:

What is my goal?

Why is this my goal?

What are my action steps?

What are my resources?

When do I want to reach my goal by?

Other Thoughts:

RECOVERY WELLNESS COACHING PLAN

Wellness Area:

What is my goal?

Why is this my goal?

What are my action steps?

What are my resources?

When do I want to reach my goal by?

Other Thoughts:

Suggested Wellness Areas:

- Overall Recovery & Wellness
- Spiritual / Purpose
- Emotional
- Community / Connection
- Family / Relationship
- Job / Career
- Physical
- Financial
- Continuing Education
- Living Environment
- Recreational / Hobby
- Other

RECOVERY WELLNESS COACHING PLAN

Suggested Wellness Areas:

- Overall Recovery & Wellness
- Spiritual / Purpose
- Emotional
- Community / Connection
- Family / Relationship
- Job / Career
- Physical
- Financial
- Continuing Education
- Living Environment
- Recreational / Hobby
- Other

Wellness Area:

What is my goal?

Why is this my goal?

What are my action steps?

What are my resources?

When do I want to reach my goal by?

Other Thoughts:

RECOVERY WELLNESS COACHING PLAN

Wellness Area:

What is my goal?

Why is this my goal?

What are my action steps?

What are my resources?

When do I want to reach my goal by?

Other Thoughts:

Suggested Wellness Areas:
- Overall Recovery & Wellness
- Spiritual / Purpose
- Emotional
- Community / Connection
- Family / Relationship
- Job / Career
- Physical
- Financial
- Continuing Education
- Living Environment
- Recreational / Hobby
- Other

RECOVERY WELLNESS COACHING PLAN

Suggested Wellness Areas:

- Overall Recovery & Wellness
- Spiritual / Purpose
- Emotional
- Community / Connection
- Family / Relationship
- Job / Career
- Physical
- Financial
- Continuing Education
- Living Environment
- Recreational / Hobby
- Other

Wellness Area:

What is my goal?

Why is this my goal?

What are my action steps?

What are my resources?

When do I want to reach my goal by?

Other Thoughts:

RECOVERY WELLNESS COACHING PLAN

Wellness Area:

What is my goal?

Why is this my goal?

What are my action steps?

What are my resources?

When do I want to reach my goal by?

Other Thoughts:

Suggested Wellness Areas:

- Overall Recovery & Wellness
- Spiritual / Purpose
- Emotional
- Community / Connection
- Family / Relationship
- Job / Career
- Physical
- Financial
- Continuing Education
- Living Environment
- Recreational / Hobby
- Other

"We ourselves feel that what we are doing is just a drop in the ocean, but the ocean would be less because of that missing drop."

Mother Teresa

You are worth it.

Made in the USA
Las Vegas, NV
25 September 2021